Leadership Matters 3.0 Journal

Andy Buck

First published 2018

by John Catt Educational Ltd,
15 Riduna Park, Melton,
Woodbridge IP12 1QT

Tel: +44 (0) 1394 389850 Fax: +44 (0) 1394 386893
Email: enquiries@johncatt.com
Website: www.johncatt.com

ISBN: 978 1 911 382 90 4

Set and designed by John Catt Educational Limited

Contents

Create teams

Deliver results and get things done

Plan and organise

Section D – Leadership approach

Follow effective action with quiet reflection.
From the quiet reflection will come even more effective action.

Peter Drucker

Using your Journal

A welcome to the *Leadership Matters Journal* from Andy Buck

How you use this Journal is really up to you. You may be using it as an individual or as part of a group of leaders as a companion to Leadership Matters. Alternatively, you may be watching the leadership clips on LM Video via the leadershipmatters.org.uk website. Or you may be engaged in a combination of all three!

In any event, the idea is that the Journal will support you in reflecting upon the leadership content presented, so that you can identify what is most useful for you in the context of your current role and situation. If your experience as a school leader is anything like my own, your time is at a premium. That's why I have designed the Journal to be really flexible, quick and easy to use. I hope that just a few minutes spent thinking through the key questions on each topic will be time well spent when it comes to supporting your continued growth and development as a leader.

The Journal is broken down into a series of easy-to-navigate topics which are summarised in the contents pages. The topic numbers in the Journal are exactly the same as the topic numbers in the third edition of the Leadership Matters book and the LM Video resources on the Leadership Matters website (leadershipmatters.org.uk). If you are using the first or second edition of the Leadership Matters book, you will find a handy cross-reference to the relevant page numbers at the very beginning of each topic.

As a useful reminder, at the start of each topic in the Journal there is a summary of the key points from book or the videos followed by the opportunity to record your reflections on:

- what ideas, theories or models resonate in the context of your role;
- what steps you commit to take as a result;
- what you are going to do to ensure you make these changes happen;
- how you will review your success in implementing them.

I would recommend that you space out your engagement with each topic. Creating and sustaining effective leadership habits takes time. My advice would be to focus on one topic at a time and give yourself the chance to master each before moving onto a new area.

If you are using the Leadership Matters website, you may also have tried out one of the LM online tools such as LM Persona, LM Style or LM 360. At the end of the Journal, there are sections that may be useful in supporting you to think through what has emerged from using these tools.

Finally, at the very back of the Journal I have included a few blank templates of what I call my Checklist for Change. This is based on a couple of well-known change models that are covered in topics 34 and 35. I hope this simple checklist will help you plan in a way that ensures any new initiative you are embarking on is a great success. There is also some space for making notes or to-do lists.

So, as you continue your leadership journey, may I wish you the very best with whatever you are 'up to' and hope that however you decide to use them, this Journal, the book, the online tools and the videos will add a little something to get you thinking along the way…

Best wishes,

Andy

Topic 1: Leadership Matters overview

If you are using the first or second edition of Leadership Matters, see the following page references for the related content: **LM1 pages 14-21 LM2 pages 9-18**

Six key areas for leadership action

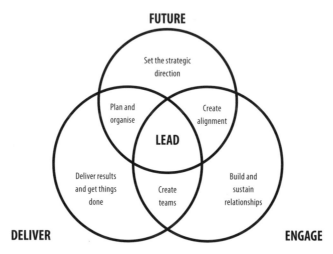

Adapted from David Pendleton's Primary Colours model combined with Steve Radcliffe's Future-Engage-Deliver

The Leadership Matters model

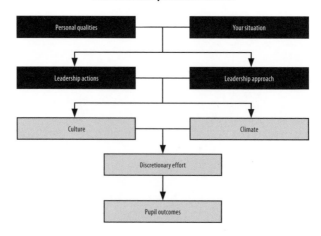

Reflection and goal-setting

Having accessed this content, what has resonated with you most strongly?

What do you want to do or change as a result?

What is the benefit for you of taking this action or making this change?
Why do you want to do it?

How will you know if you have been successful?

Planning for your success

What's the timing? By when will you have achieved it?

What or who could support you making this happen?

What or who could stop this happening?

What can you do to prevent this?

What's your very first step to start this off? When will you take it?

_____

_____

_____

_____

_____

_____

_____

Reviewing your success

What has changed for the better? What have you achieved?

_____

_____

_____

_____

_____

_____

_____

Is there anything that you would like to further improve?

_____

_____

_____

_____

_____

_____

_____

Notes

Topic 2: Discretionary effort

If you are using the first or second edition of Leadership Matters, see the following page references for the related content: **LM1 pages 18-20 LM2 pages 18-22**

Leadership and results

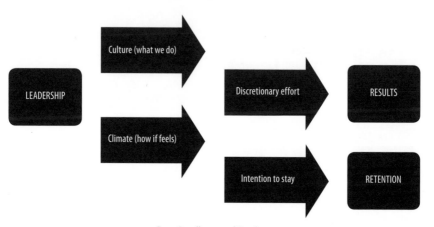

From Pendleton and Furnham

Building discretionary effort

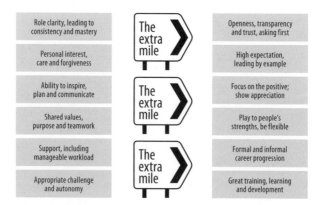

Reflection and goal-setting

Having accessed this content, what has resonated with you most strongly?

What do you want to do or change as a result?

What is the benefit for you of taking this action or making this change?
Why do you want to do it?

How will you know if you have been successful?

Planning for your success

What's the timing? By when will you have achieved it?

What or who could support you making this happen?

What or who could stop this happening?

What can you do to prevent this?

What's your very first step to start this off? When will you take it?

_____
_____
_____
_____
_____
_____

Reviewing your success
What has changed for the better? What have you achieved?

_____
_____
_____
_____
_____
_____

Is there anything that you would like to further improve?

_____
_____
_____
_____
_____
_____

Notes

Topic 3: Effective leadership development

There is no content in the first and second editions of
Leadership Matters that relates to this topic.

1. The approach distinguishes between learning and development, with both included as part of a clear pedagogical framework. It's all very well learning something, but it's only useful if that enables you to develop your practice in a sustainable way.

2. It offers evidence-based leadership knowledge within a carefully constructed curriculum that leaders can then apply within their context.

3. This leadership knowledge sits within a coherent leadership framework. Topic 1 set out the framwork we use at Leadership Matters.

4. Learning with and from peers is a key feature of the approach.

5. There is an implicit understanding that leadership habits and skills take time to develop, and programme length reflects this.

6. An appropriate blend of teaching, mentoring, coaching, personal reflection and goal-setting are an integral part of the approach.

7. Tools that support self-awareness such as personality predisposition and 360 feedback are available towards the start of the process. That is why we have created LM Persona, LM Style and LM 360 on the Leadership Matters website.

8. There is an opportunity through carefully curated publications and online resources for participants to personalise their learning. To support with this, in addition to LM Video, we have created LM Insight, a part of the Leadership Matters that contains links to the very best leadership articles, videos and diagnostic tools on the web.

9. There is a focus on the evaluation of impact throughout the process.

10. The overall approach should stretch, support and challenge leaders, leaving them feeling empowered and positive about the future.

5 Es model for learning and development

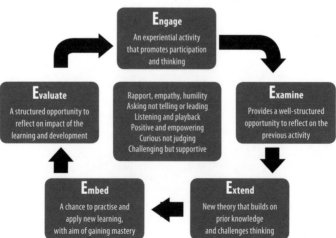

Reflection and goal-setting

Having accessed this content, what has resonated with you most strongly?

What do you want to do or change as a result?

What is the benefit for you of taking this action or making this change? Why do you want to do it?

How will you know if you have been successful?

Planning for your success

What's the timing? By when will you have achieved it?

What or who could support you making this happen?

What or who could stop this happening?

What can you do to prevent this?

What's your very first step to start this off? When will you take it?

Reviewing your success
What has changed for the better? What have you achieved?

Is there anything that you would like to further improve?

Notes

Topic 4: Leadership Matters resources

If you are using the first or second edition of Leadership Matters, see the following page references for the related content: **LM1 n/a LM2 pages 201-203**

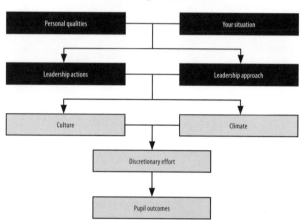

The Leadership Matters model

LMBOOKS

Opportunity to buy LM books, journal (and more) at a discount

LMVIDEO

40 videos by Andy Buck, linked to the book and journal topics

LMPRESENT

40 downloadable PPT slide sets, linked to the 40 LM Videos

LMINSIGHT

The best leadership articles, tools and videos from the web

LMPERSONA

Gain valuable insights into your leadership predispositions

LM360

Chance for leaders to self-reflect and get peer feedback

LMSTYLE

Discover leadership styles you tend to use and those you don't

LMSURVEY

Easy way to gather feedback from pupils, staff and parents

LMTEMPLATE

Downloadable WORD and EXCEL docs to support leaders

LMPEOPLE

Easy way to contact great speakers, trainers and coaches

LMMEET

Six regional events hosted by Andy Buck for LM members

LMINITIATIVES

Supporting the education of girls in the developing world

Reflection and goal-setting

Having accessed this content, what has resonated with you most strongly?

What do you want to do or change as a result?

What is the benefit for you of taking this action or making this change?
Why do you want to do it?

How will you know if you have been successful?

Planning for your success

What's the timing? By when will you have achieved it?

What or who could support you making this happen?

What or who could stop this happening?

What can you do to prevent this?

What's your very first step to start this off? When will you take it?

_____

_____

_____

_____

_____

_____

_____

Reviewing your success

What has changed for the better? What have you achieved?

_____

_____

_____

_____

_____

_____

Is there anything that you would like to further improve?

_____

_____

_____

_____

_____

_____

Notes

Topic 5: Emotional intelligence

If you are using the first or second edition of Leadership Matters, see the following page references for the related content: **LM1 pages 32-34 LM2 pages 35-37**

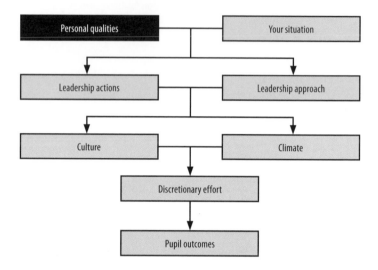

A model of emotional intelligence

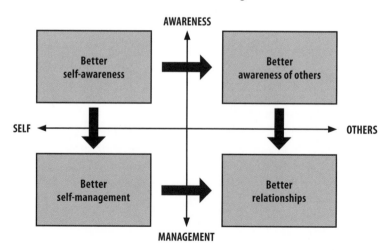

Daniel Goleman

Reflection and goal-setting

Having accessed this content, what has resonated with you most strongly?

What do you want to do or change as a result?

What is the benefit for you of taking this action or making this change?
Why do you want to do it?

How will you know if you have been successful?

Planning for your success

What's the timing? By when will you have achieved it?

What or who could support you making this happen?

What or who could stop this happening?

What can you do to prevent this?

What's your very first step to start this off? When will you take it?

Reviewing your success
What has changed for the better? What have you achieved?

Is there anything that you would like to further improve?

Notes

Topic 6: Self-awareness and predisposition

If you are using the first or second edition of Leadership Matters, see the following page references for the related content: **LM1 pages 25-32 LM2 pages 27-35**

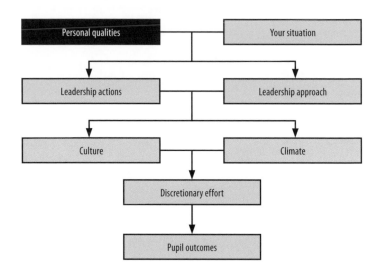

The Johari window

	Known to self	Not known to self
Known to others	**OPEN**	**BLIND SPOT**
Not known to others	**HIDDEN**	**UNKNOWN**

Luft and Ingham

Reflection and goal-setting

Having accessed this content, what has resonated with you most strongly?

What do you want to do or change as a result?

What is the benefit for you of taking this action or making this change?
Why do you want to do it?

How will you know if you have been successful?

Planning for your success

What's the timing? By when will you have achieved it?

What or who could support you making this happen?

What or who could stop this happening?

What can you do to prevent this?

What's your very first step to start this off? When will you take it?

_____

_____

_____

_____

_____

_____

Reviewing your success
What has changed for the better? What have you achieved?

_____

_____

_____

_____

_____

_____

Is there anything that you would like to further improve?

_____

_____

_____

_____

_____

_____

Notes

Topic 7: Courage and resilience

If you are using the first or second edition of Leadership Matters, see the following page references for the related content: **LM1 pages 35-41 LM2 pages 39-45**

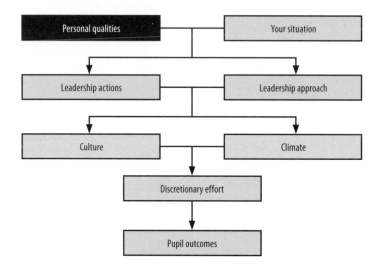

A model for resilience

CONFIDENCE

1. Self-belief
2. Coping with stressful situations
3. Right balance of positive and negative emotions

SOCIAL SUPPORT

1. Good relationship with others
2. Willingness to seek support
3. Knowing when to draw on the support

ADAPTABILITY

1. Able to cope with change, particularly when imposed
2. Flexible when needed
3. Can recover quickly in such situations

PURPOSEFULNESS

1. Clear sense of purpose in role
2. Strong values, drive and direction
3. Achieve in the face of setbacks

Adapted from Robertson Cooper

Reflection and goal-setting

Having accessed this content, what has resonated with you most strongly?

What do you want to do or change as a result?

What is the benefit for you of taking this action or making this change?
Why do you want to do it?

How will you know if you have been successful?

Planning for your success

What's the timing? By when will you have achieved it?

_____

_____

_____

_____

_____

_____

_____

What or who could support you making this happen?

_____

_____

_____

_____

_____

_____

_____

What or who could stop this happening?

_____

_____

_____

_____

_____

_____

_____

What can you do to prevent this?

_____

_____

_____

_____

_____

_____

_____

What's your very first step to start this off? When will you take it?

_____

_____

_____

_____

_____

_____

_____

Reviewing your success
What has changed for the better? What have you achieved?

_____

_____

_____

_____

_____

_____

Is there anything that you would like to further improve?

_____

_____

_____

_____

_____

_____

Notes

Topic 8: Humility

If you are using the first or second edition of Leadership Matters, see the following page references for the related content: **LM1 pages 43-46 LM2 pages 47-52**

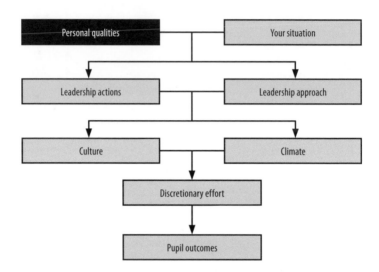

Humility is not thinking less of yourself, but thinking of yourself less.

C.S. Lewis

Reflection and goal-setting

Having accessed this content, what has resonated with you most strongly?

What do you want to do or change as a result?

What is the benefit for you of taking this action or making this change?
Why do you want to do it?

How will you know if you have been successful?

Planning for your success
What's the timing? By when will you have achieved it?

What or who could support you making this happen?

What or who could stop this happening?

What can you do to prevent this?

What's your very first step to start this off? When will you take it?

_____
_____
_____
_____
_____
_____
_____

Reviewing your success
What has changed for the better? What have you achieved?

_____
_____
_____
_____
_____
_____

Is there anything that you would like to further improve?

_____
_____
_____
_____
_____
_____

Notes

Topic 9: Context

If you are using the first or second edition of Leadership Matters, see the following page references for the related content: **LM1 pages 55-60 LM2 pages 59-66**

Reliability of lesson observations

		Probability that 2nd rater disagrees	
1st rater gives	**%**	*Best case* *r = 0.7*	*Worst case* *r = 0.24*
Outstanding	12%	51%	78%
Good	55%	31%	43%
Req. Impr.	29%	46%	64%
Inadequate	4%	62%	90%
Overall		**39%**	**55%**

Percentages based on simulations

Adapted by Rob Coe based on the work of Michal Strong

The ladder of inference

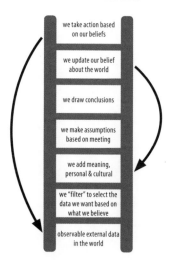

Argyris and Senge

Reflection and goal-setting

Having accessed this content, what has resonated with you most strongly?

What do you want to do or change as a result?

What is the benefit for you of taking this action or making this change?
Why do you want to do it?

How will you know if you have been successful?

Planning for your success

What's the timing? By when will you have achieved it?

What or who could support you making this happen?

What or who could stop this happening?

What can you do to prevent this?

What's your very first step to start this off? When will you take it?

_____

_____

_____

_____

_____

_____

Reviewing your success
What has changed for the better? What have you achieved?

_____

_____

_____

_____

_____

Is there anything that you would like to further improve?

_____

_____

_____

_____

_____

_____

Notes

Topic 10: Monitoring and data

If you are using the first or second edition of Leadership Matters, see the following page references for the related content: **LM1 pages 129-130; 143-144 LM2 pages 142-143; 157-159.**

Hay group

✓ a clear 'why'
✓ owned by teachers
✓ owned by pupils
✓ focus on progress
✓ identify individuals
✓ identify groups
✓ question-level analysis
✓ SoW and pedagogy
✓ focused intervention

Reflection and goal-setting

Having accessed this content, what has resonated with you most strongly?

What do you want to do or change as a result?

What is the benefit for you of taking this action or making this change?
Why do you want to do it?

How will you know if you have been successful?

Planning for your success

What's the timing? By when will you have achieved it?

What or who could support you making this happen?

What or who could stop this happening?

What can you do to prevent this?

What's your very first step to start this off? When will you take it?

Reviewing your success
What has changed for the better? What have you achieved?

Is there anything that you would like to further improve?

Notes

Topic 11: Performance and predispositions

There is no content in the first and second editions of
Leadership Matters that relates to this topic.

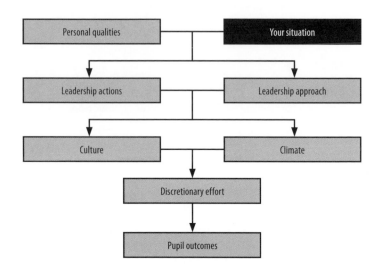

Playing to strengths

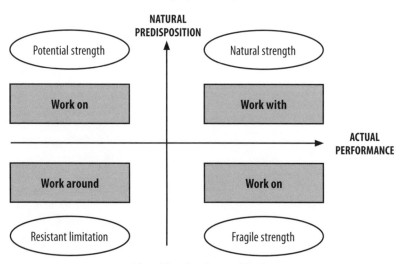

Adapted from Pendleton and Furnham

Reflection and goal-setting

Having accessed this content, what has resonated with you most strongly?

What do you want to do or change as a result?

What is the benefit for you of taking this action or making this change?
Why do you want to do it?

How will you know if you have been successful?

Planning for your success

What's the timing? By when will you have achieved it?

What or who could support you making this happen?

What or who could stop this happening?

What can you do to prevent this?

What's your very first step to start this off? When will you take it?

Reviewing your success
What has changed for the better? What have you achieved?

Is there anything that you would like to further improve?

Notes

Topic 12: Performance, behaviours and values

If you are using the first or second edition of Leadership Matters, see the following page references for the related content: **LM1 pages 49-54 LM2 pages 53-58**

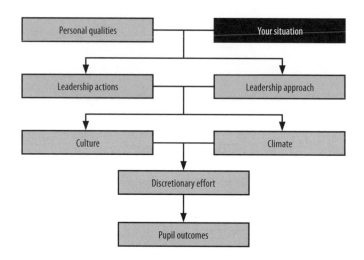

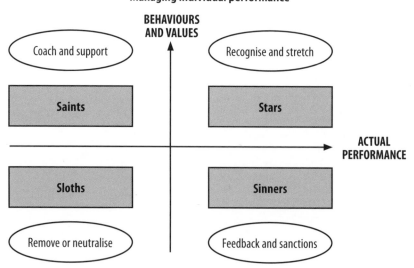

Adapted from Pendleton and Furnham

Reflection and goal-setting

Having accessed this content, what has resonated with you most strongly?

What do you want to do or change as a result?

What is the benefit for you of taking this action or making this change? Why do you want to do it?

How will you know if you have been successful?

Planning for your success

What's the timing? By when will you have achieved it?

What or who could support you making this happen?

What or who could stop this happening?

What can you do to prevent this?

What's your very first step to start this off? When will you take it?

Reviewing your success
What has changed for the better? What have you achieved?

Is there anything that you would like to further improve?

Notes

Topic 13: Vision, values and strategy

If you are using the first or second edition of Leadership Matters, see the following page references for the related content: **LM1 pages 61-74 LM2 pages 67-84**

Start with why

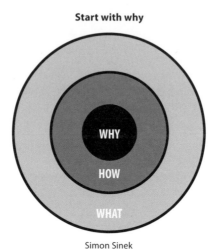

Simon Sinek

OST

Objectives (ideally just 2 or 3 in any given year; maximum of 6; need to be SMART)
• Increase the number of pupils getting to university to 160 by 2022
Strategy (only one for each objective)
• Building independence and a growth mindset
Tactics (linked to each strategy – keep as simple as possible)
• Praise effort and process • Stop using extrinsic rewards such as Vivo points • Organise university trips in Years 7, 9 and 12 • Bring successful former pupils back in Years 8, 10, 11 and 13 to inspire pupils • Develop extended project approach from Year 7, embedded x-curricular • Provide wide co-curricular opportunities, including sports, arts, travel, adventure, debating, volunteering, camps • Organise inspirational visiting speakers who grew up locally

Adapted from Alistair Campbell in *Winners*

Reflection and goal-setting

Having accessed this content, what has resonated with you most strongly?

What do you want to do or change as a result?

What is the benefit for you of taking this action or making this change?
Why do you want to do it?

How will you know if you have been successful?

Planning for your success
What's the timing? By when will you have achieved it?

What or who could support you making this happen?

What or who could stop this happening?

What can you do to prevent this?

What's your very first step to start this off? When will you take it?

Reviewing your success
What has changed for the better? What have you achieved?

Is there anything that you would like to further improve?

Notes

Topic 14: Leading for maximum impact

If you are using the first or second edition of Leadership Matters, see the following page references for the related content: **LM1 pages 150-151 LM2 pages 164-165**

Six key areas for leadership action

What it is leaders do that has the biggest impact on pupil outcomes

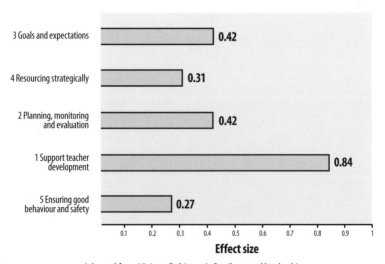

Adapted from Viviane Robinson's *Pupil-centred leadership*

Reflection and goal-setting

Having accessed this content, what has resonated with you most strongly?

What do you want to do or change as a result?

What is the benefit for you of taking this action or making this change? Why do you want to do it?

How will you know if you have been successful?

Planning for your success

What's the timing? By when will you have achieved it?

What or who could support you making this happen?

What or who could stop this happening?

What can you do to prevent this?

What's your very first step to start this off? When will you take it?

_____

_____

_____

_____

_____

_____

Reviewing your success
What has changed for the better? What have you achieved?

_____

_____

_____

_____

_____

_____

Is there anything that you would like to further improve?

_____

_____

_____

_____

_____

_____

Notes

Topic 15: Pupil self-belief and motivation

There is no content in the first and second editions of
Leadership Matters that relates to this topic.

Six key areas for leadership action

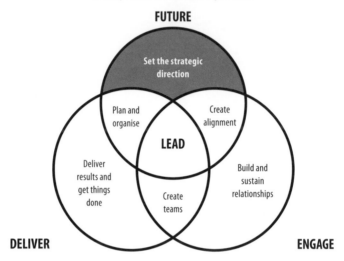

Building self-belief and motivation

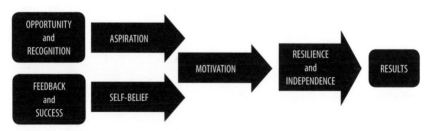

Reflection and goal-setting

Having accessed this content, what has resonated with you most strongly?

What do you want to do or change as a result?

What is the benefit for you of taking this action or making this change?
Why do you want to do it?

How will you know if you have been successful?

Planning for your success

What's the timing? By when will you have achieved it?

_____

_____

_____

_____

_____

_____

What or who could support you making this happen?

_____

_____

_____

_____

_____

_____

What or who could stop this happening?

_____

_____

_____

_____

_____

_____

What can you do to prevent this?

_____

_____

_____

_____

_____

_____

What's your very first step to start this off? When will you take it?

Reviewing your success
What has changed for the better? What have you achieved?

Is there anything that you would like to further improve?

Notes

Topic 16: Decision-making

If you are using the first or second edition of Leadership Matters, see the following page references for the related content: **LM1 no content LM2 pages 80-84**

Common types of decision-making bias

Bias	Definition
Anchoring	The tendency to rely too heavily, or 'anchor', on a past reference or on one trait or piece of information when making decisions.
Availability heuristic	Estimating what is more likely by what is more available in memory, which is biased toward vivid, unusual, or emotionally charged examples.
Endowment effect	The fact that people often demand much more to give up an object than they would be willing to pay to acquire it. Also connected with the 'status quo' bias.
Framing effect	Drawing different conclusions from the same information, depending on how that information is presented.
Gambler's fallacy	The tendency to think that future probabilities are altered by past events, when in reality they are unchanged.
Group think	Peer pressure to conform to the opinions held by the group.
Optimism	The tendency to be over-optimistic, over-estimating favourable and pleasing outcomes.

Q-Learning

The STOP model

Situation
Have you properly understood the situation? What additional information would it be useful to acquire before you make a decision?

Temptations
What is the potential to make a biased decision? In particular, how are you making sure you aren't making a decision based on an emotional response?

Options
What are your options? Take some time to think through other ideas, not just doing the first thing you think of. What else could you do?

Plan
This could be as simple as a short to-do list or a more complex plan, depending on what is involved.

Reflection and goal-setting

Having accessed this content, what has resonated with you most strongly?

What do you want to do or change as a result?

What is the benefit for you of taking this action or making this change?
Why do you want to do it?

How will you know if you have been successful?

Planning for your success

What's the timing? By when will you have achieved it?

_____
_____
_____
_____
_____
_____
_____

What or who could support you making this happen?

_____
_____
_____
_____
_____
_____

What or who could stop this happening?

_____
_____
_____
_____
_____
_____

What can you do to prevent this?

_____
_____
_____
_____
_____
_____

What's your very first step to start this off? When will you take it?

Reviewing your success
What has changed for the better? What have you achieved?

Is there anything that you would like to further improve?

Notes

Topic 17: Clarity

If you are using the first or second edition of Leadership Matters, see the following page references for the related content: **LM1 pages 75-86 LM2 pages 85-92**

Six key areas for leadership action

FUTURE

Set the strategic direction

Plan and organise

Create alignment

LEAD

Deliver results and get things done

Create teams

Build and sustain relationships

DELIVER

ENGAGE

The giraffe concept (see Topic 1 in Leadership Matters 3.0 book)

Reflection and goal-setting

Having accessed this content, what has resonated with you most strongly?

What do you want to do or change as a result?

What is the benefit for you of taking this action or making this change? Why do you want to do it?

How will you know if you have been successful?

Planning for your success

What's the timing? By when will you have achieved it?

What or who could support you making this happen?

What or who could stop this happening?

What can you do to prevent this?

What's your very first step to start this off? When will you take it?

_____

_____

_____

_____

_____

_____

_____

Reviewing your success
What has changed for the better? What have you achieved?

_____

_____

_____

_____

_____

_____

Is there anything that you would like to further improve?

_____

_____

_____

_____

_____

_____

Notes

Topic 18: Influencing others

If you are using the first or second edition of Leadership Matters, see the following page references for the related content: **LM1 pages 79-82 LM2 pages 89-92**

Six key areas for leadership action

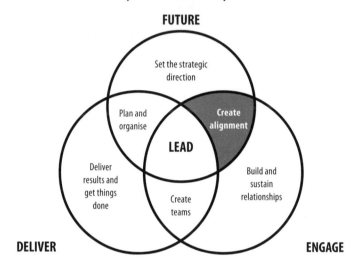

- ✓ Know them; build rapport
- ✓ Understand their context
- ✓ Your credibility; build trust
- ✓ Clarity of your goal
- ✓ Address their concerns
- ✓ Solve their problems
- ✓ Leave them positive

Reflection and goal-setting

Having accessed this content, what has resonated with you most strongly?

What do you want to do or change as a result?

What is the benefit for you of taking this action or making this change?
Why do you want to do it?

How will you know if you have been successful?

Planning for your success
What's the timing? By when will you have achieved it?

_____
_____
_____
_____
_____
_____
_____

What or who could support you making this happen?

_____
_____
_____
_____
_____
_____
_____

What or who could stop this happening?

_____
_____
_____
_____
_____
_____
_____

What can you do to prevent this?

_____
_____
_____
_____
_____
_____
_____

What's your very first step to start this off? When will you take it?

Reviewing your success
What has changed for the better? What have you achieved?

Is there anything that you would like to further improve?

Notes

Topic 19: Managing up

If you are using the first or second edition of Leadership Matters, see the following page references for the related content: **LM1 pages 82-85 LM2 pages 92-94**

Six key areas for leadership action

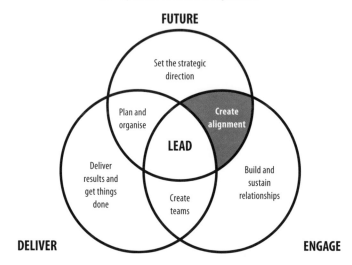

Managing up

Checklist		Yes	No
1	I am aware of my manager's expectations of me and have articulated my expectations of my boss.		
2	I regularly inform my manager of what I'm working on.		
3	I notify my manager of problems promptly and suggest several solutions to consider.		
4	My boss and I deal with disagreements as they arise.		
5	My relationship with my manager is characterised by trust and reliability.		
6	I understand my boss's pressures and priorities.		
7	My manager never steps in to direct one or more of my employees.		
8	I've asked my manager openly about his or her management style and likes and dislikes and have adapted my style to my boss's as much as possible.		
9	I take as much time as necessary to communicate with my manager about important matters.		
10	I seek ways to exert my influence on the other leaders so as to support my manager's goals.		
	Total number of ticks		

Reflection and goal-setting

Having accessed this content, what has resonated with you most strongly?

What do you want to do or change as a result?

What is the benefit for you of taking this action or making this change? Why do you want to do it?

How will you know if you have been successful?

Planning for your success

What's the timing? By when will you have achieved it?

What or who could support you making this happen?

What or who could stop this happening?

What can you do to prevent this?

What's your very first step to start this off? When will you take it?

_____
_____
_____
_____
_____
_____
_____

Reviewing your success
What has changed for the better? What have you achieved?

_____
_____
_____
_____
_____
_____

Is there anything that you would like to further improve?

_____
_____
_____
_____
_____
_____

Notes

Topic 20: Inspection and review

If you are using the first or second edition of Leadership Matters, see the following page references for the related content: **LM1 no content LM2 pages 95-97**

JEFI: a model for aligning thinking during external review

Judgement

- Is it outstanding, good, RI or inadequate?
- How secure is the judgement?

Evidence

- What is your evidence for the judgement?
- How has this been validated?

Focus

- What are the current priorities in this area?
- Why are you focusing on these?

Impact

- What has been their impact so far?
- How do you know?

A template for using JEFI

	J Judgement	E Evidence	F Focus	I Impact
Leadership and management				
Teaching, learning and assessment				
Personal dev, behaviour and welfare				
Outcomes for pupils				

Reflection and goal-setting

Having accessed this content, what has resonated with you most strongly?

What do you want to do or change as a result?

What is the benefit for you of taking this action or making this change? Why do you want to do it?

How will you know if you have been successful?

Planning for your success

What's the timing? By when will you have achieved it?

What or who could support you making this happen?

What or who could stop this happening?

What can you do to prevent this?

What's your very first step to start this off? When will you take it?

Reviewing your success
What has changed for the better? What have you achieved?

Is there anything that you would like to further improve?

Notes

Topic 21: Transparency and trust

If you are using the first or second edition of Leadership Matters, see the following page references for the related content: **LM1 pages 163-170 LM2 pages 179-188**

Six key areas for leadership action

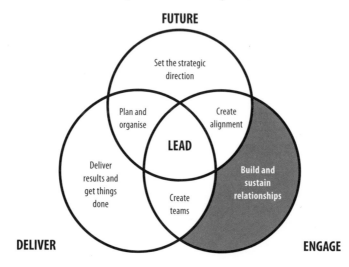

The key elements of trust

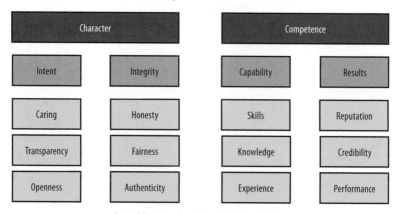

Adapted from Stephen Covey's *The Speed of Trust*

Reflection and goal-setting

Having accessed this content, what has resonated with you most strongly?

What do you want to do or change as a result?

What is the benefit for you of taking this action or making this change? Why do you want to do it?

How will you know if you have been successful?

Planning for your success

What's the timing? By when will you have achieved it?

What or who could support you making this happen?

What or who could stop this happening?

What can you do to prevent this?

What's your very first step to start this off? When will you take it?

Reviewing your success
What has changed for the better? What have you achieved?

Is there anything that you would like to further improve?

Notes

Topic 22: Little things matter

If you are using the first or second edition of Leadership Matters, see the following page references for the related content: **LM1 pages 98-99 LM2 pages 110-111**

Six key areas for leadership action

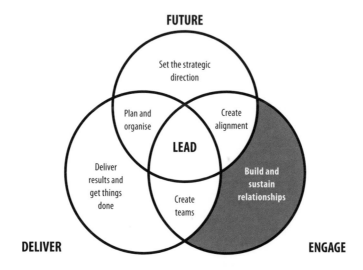

	If you have something good to say, why not write it?
	If you have an issue, always try to speak face to face
	Keep promises
	Keep confidences

Reflection and goal-setting

Having accessed this content, what has resonated with you most strongly?

What do you want to do or change as a result?

What is the benefit for you of taking this action or making this change?
Why do you want to do it?

How will you know if you have been successful?

Planning for your success

What's the timing? By when will you have achieved it?

What or who could support you making this happen?

What or who could stop this happening?

What can you do to prevent this?

What's your very first step to start this off? When will you take it?

Reviewing your success
What has changed for the better? What have you achieved?

Is there anything that you would like to further improve?

Notes

Topic 23: Managing conflict

If you are using the first or second edition of Leadership Matters, see the following page references for the related content: **LM1 pages 94-97 LM2 pages 106-109**

Six key areas for leadership action

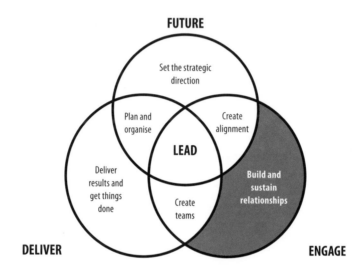

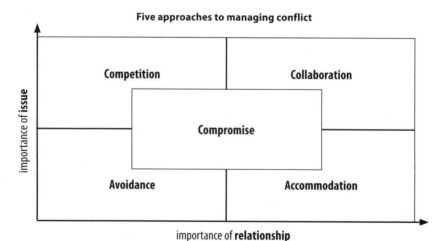

Five approaches to managing conflict

Thomas Kilmann

Reflection and goal-setting

Having accessed this content, what has resonated with you most strongly?

What do you want to do or change as a result?

What is the benefit for you of taking this action or making this change?
Why do you want to do it?

How will you know if you have been successful?

Planning for your success

What's the timing? By when will you have achieved it?

What or who could support you making this happen?

What or who could stop this happening?

What can you do to prevent this?

What's your very first step to start this off? When will you take it?

Reviewing your success
What has changed for the better? What have you achieved?

Is there anything that you would like to further improve?

Notes

Topic 24: External partnerships

If you are using the first or second edition of Leadership Matters, see the following page references for the related content: **LM1 pages 92-94 LM2 pages 104-105**

Auditing your partnership

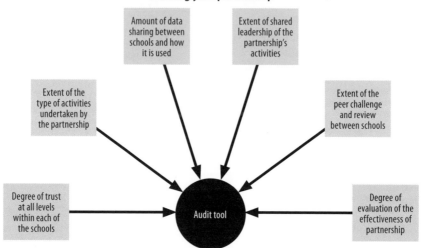

Amount of data sharing between schools and how it is used

Extent of shared leadership of the partnership's activities

Extent of the type of activities undertaken by the partnership

Extent of the peer challenge and review between schools

Degree of trust at all levels within each of the schools

Audit tool

Degree of evaluation of the effectiveness of partnership

Based on a think-piece by David Hargreaves

Key features of successful MATs

- ✓ An ability to recruit and retain powerful and authoritative executive leaders, with a clear vision for bringing about higher standards
- ✓ A well-planned, broad and balanced curriculum that equips pupils with a strong command of the basics of English and mathematics, as well as the confidence, ambition and team-work skills to succeed in later life
- ✓ A commitment to provide a high-quality education for all pupils, in a calm and scholarly atmosphere
- ✓ Investment in professional development of teachers and the sharing of knowledge and expertise across a strong network of constituent schools
- ✓ A high priority given to initial teacher training and leadership development to secure a pipeline of future talent
- ✓ Clear frameworks of governance, accountability and delegation
- ✓ Effective use of assessment information to identify, escalate and tackle problems quickly
- ✓ A cautious and considered approach to expansion

House of Commons

Reflection and goal-setting

Having accessed this content, what has resonated with you most strongly?

What do you want to do or change as a result?

What is the benefit for you of taking this action or making this change? Why do you want to do it?

How will you know if you have been successful?

Planning for your success

What's the timing? By when will you have achieved it?

_____

What or who could support you making this happen?

_____

What or who could stop this happening?

_____

What can you do to prevent this?

_____

What's your very first step to start this off? When will you take it?

Reviewing your success
What has changed for the better? What have you achieved?

Is there anything that you would like to further improve?

Notes

Topic 25: Teams and teamwork

If you are using the first or second edition of Leadership Matters, see the following page references for the related content: **LM1 pages 101-116 LM2 pages 113-128**

Six key areas for leadership action

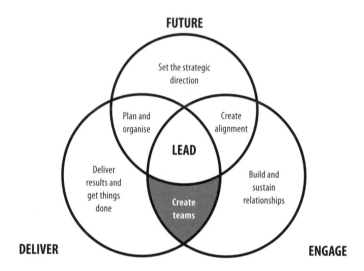

A model for team development

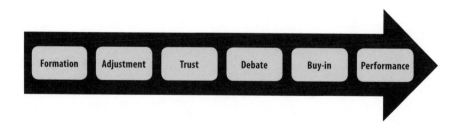

Reflection and goal-setting

Having accessed this content, what has resonated with you most strongly?

What do you want to do or change as a result?

What is the benefit for you of taking this action or making this change?
Why do you want to do it?

How will you know if you have been successful?

Planning for your success

What's the timing? By when will you have achieved it?

What or who could support you making this happen?

What or who could stop this happening?

What can you do to prevent this?

What's your very first step to start this off? When will you take it?

_____
_____
_____
_____
_____
_____

Reviewing your success
What has changed for the better? What have you achieved?

_____
_____
_____
_____
_____
_____

Is there anything that you would like to further improve?

_____
_____
_____
_____
_____
_____

Notes

Topic 26: Delegation

If you are using the first or second edition of Leadership Matters, see the following page references for the related content: **LM1 pages 110-115 LM2 pages 123-128**

Nine levels of delegation

1. Look into this problem. Give me all the facts. I will decide what to do.
2. Let me know the alternatives available, with the pros and cons of each. I will decide what to select.
3. Let me know the criteria for your recommendation, which alternatives you have identified and which one appears best to you, with any risk identified. I will make the decision.
4. Recommend a course of action for my approval.
5. Let me know what you intend to do. Delay action until I approve.
6. Let me know what you intend to do. Do it unless I say not to.
7. Take action. Let me know what you did. Let me know how it turns out.
8. Take action. Communicate with me only if your action is unsuccessful.
9. Take action. No further communication with me is necessary.

Tim Brighouse

Top tips for effective delegation

1. When you delegate, make sure the other person is **set up to succeed** because they have the capacity and competence (with support, if needed) to achieve the task.
2. Make sure there is **clarity** about what is required, by when and to what standard. People usually don't know all the detail you have in your head.
3. **Be patient**. Remember that to start with it is unlikely that the person you are delegating to will carry out the task as well or as fast as you would.
4. Don't assume how much the person wants you to keep close to the task. Have a conversation. This will avoid them thinking you are either micro-managing or, at the other extreme, that you have abdicated your responsibility. **Agree with them** the frequency and nature of check-in points.
5. **Don't underestimate** what people are keen or able to take on. Usually people are pleased to be asked, especially if you are playing to people's strengths or stretching them.
6. Make sure the people you delegate to have the **authority and resource** to get the job done. And don't just delegate all the **boring jobs** or those you'd rather not do.
7. Make sure you **plan ahead** and give people plenty of time, rather than using delegation only when you are under pressure for time yourself.
8. Make sure you **don't delegate high risk or critical projects** unless you are 100% sure the person can deliver them. It isn't fair to put someone under that pressure.
9. When you delegate, think about **who else can help** or what the interdependencies of the work might be. Might it be something to delegate to a team rather than a person?
10. Make sure you say **thanks** for a job well done!

Reflection and goal-setting

Having accessed this content, what has resonated with you most strongly?

What do you want to do or change as a result?

What is the benefit for you of taking this action or making this change? Why do you want to do it?

How will you know if you have been successful?

Planning for your success

What's the timing? By when will you have achieved it?

What or who could support you making this happen?

What or who could stop this happening?

What can you do to prevent this?

What's your very first step to start this off? When will you take it?

_____

_____

_____

_____

_____

_____

_____

Reviewing your success
What has changed for the better? What have you achieved?

_____

_____

_____

_____

_____

_____

Is there anything that you would like to further improve?

_____

_____

_____

_____

_____

_____

Notes

Topic 27: Team meetings

If you are using the first or second edition of Leadership Matters, see the following page references for the related content: **LM1 pages 103-106 LM2 pages 116-120**

Top tips for effective meetings

1. Be clear what type of meeting it is – **what is it for**?
2. Make sure the **environment** is right; offer refreshments?
3. Don't have a meeting for the **sake of it**
4. Make sure the **right people** are there; use sub-groups
5. Ensure there is plenty of **notice** of meetings and pre-work
6. Have a **clear agenda** (prioritised; realistic; timed; owned)
7. Agree **meeting protocols** for discussion and stick to them
8. Usually best **not to 'present'** anything – send out pre-reading (in good time) and assume it has been read properly
9. Keep a clear **record** of agreed actions
10. **Chair** should: encourage participation; keep focus; keep to time
11. Mobile technology **protocols** are clear and followed
12. **Rotate** roles of chair and note-taker, where appropriate
13. Clarify **outcomes** at the end and thank everyone
14. Share note of meeting **promptly**, with actions, owners and timelines
    Use **pre- and post-meeting** discussions to 'oil the wheels'
15. **Participants** should listen, respect others' views, be honest, challenge constructively, respect confidentiality and adhere to cabinet responsibility

Reflection and goal-setting

Having accessed this content, what has resonated with you most strongly?

What do you want to do or change as a result?

What is the benefit for you of taking this action or making this change?
Why do you want to do it?

How will you know if you have been successful?

Planning for your success

What's the timing? By when will you have achieved it?

What or who could support you making this happen?

What or who could stop this happening?

What can you do to prevent this?

What's your very first step to start this off? When will you take it?

_____
_____
_____
_____
_____
_____

Reviewing your success
What has changed for the better? What have you achieved?

_____
_____
_____
_____
_____

Is there anything that you would like to further improve?

_____
_____
_____
_____
_____

Notes

Topic 28: 1:1 meetings

If you are using the first or second edition of Leadership Matters, see the following page references for the related content: **LM1 pages 101-103 LM2 pages 113-115**

Top tips for great 1:1 meetings

1. Agree or **contract** with one another at the start how your 1:1s will work.
2. **Schedule** your 1:1s well in advance and avoid cancelling.
3. As you delegate more, let your team members each **create their own agenda** (maybe provide an agenda template to help) – add in your items afterwards. Decide if you will settle the agenda **before or in** the meeting.
4. Avoid the temptation for them to be updates – this can often be done in other ways. Try to make your 1:1s about things that need **discussion**.
5. Ask **questions** more than you give advice. Make your 1:1s **developmental**.
6. Occasionally, **ask for help** with something you are working on that you would value their opinion or help with.
7. Make your 1:1s feel **personal**. Ask them how you can do this.
8. Try to ensure they **leave feeling** valued, energised and positive.
9. If you have any follow-up actions, try to do them the **same day** if you can.
10. Occasionally, **ask for feedback** on your own performance.

Suggested format for updates

Area of work	Success criteria	Update
High level descriptor	How will I know it has been achieved?	Including how 'on track' the item is and highlighting anything it would be useful to discuss

Reflection and goal-setting

Having accessed this content, what has resonated with you most strongly?

What do you want to do or change as a result?

What is the benefit for you of taking this action or making this change? Why do you want to do it?

How will you know if you have been successful?

Planning for your success

What's the timing? By when will you have achieved it?

What or who could support you making this happen?

What or who could stop this happening?

What can you do to prevent this?

What's your very first step to start this off? When will you take it?

_____

_____

_____

_____

_____

_____

Reviewing your success
What has changed for the better? What have you achieved?

_____

_____

_____

_____

_____

Is there anything that you would like to further improve?

_____

_____

_____

_____

_____

Notes

Topic 29: Consistency

If you are using the first or second edition of Leadership Matters, see the following page references for the related content: **LM1 pages 75-82 and 117-121 LM2 pages 85-92 and 129-133**

Six key areas for leadership action

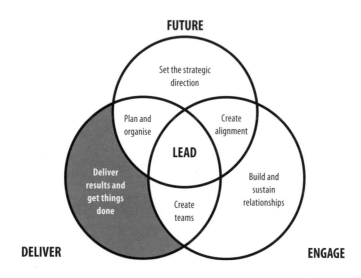

Action without vision is only passing time. Vision without action is merely daydreaming. But vision with action can change the world.

Nelson Mandela

Reflection and goal-setting

Having accessed this content, what has resonated with you most strongly?

What do you want to do or change as a result?

What is the benefit for you of taking this action or making this change? Why do you want to do it?

How will you know if you have been successful?

Planning for your success

What's the timing? By when will you have achieved it?

_____

_____

_____

_____

_____

_____

_____

What or who could support you making this happen?

_____

_____

_____

_____

_____

_____

What or who could stop this happening?

_____

_____

_____

_____

_____

_____

What can you do to prevent this?

_____

_____

_____

_____

_____

_____

What's your very first step to start this off? When will you take it?

_____

_____

_____

_____

_____

_____

Reviewing your success
What has changed for the better? What have you achieved?

_____

_____

_____

_____

_____

Is there anything that you would like to further improve?

_____

_____

_____

_____

_____

Notes

Topic 30: Incremental coaching

If you are using the first or second edition of Leadership Matters, see the following page references for the related content: **LM1 pages 124-126 LM2 pages 136-139**

Five errors to avoid when it comes to helping teachers improve

Error 1: More is better.

Top-tier Truth: *Less is more.* Many leaders fall prey to the temptation to deliver feedback on every aspect of the lesson. While that is a useful tool to demonstrate your instructional expertise, it won't change practice nearly as effectively. As we can learn from coaches in every field, bite-sized feedback on just one or two areas delivers the most effective improvement.

Error 2: Lengthy written evaluations drive change as effectively as any other form of feedback.

Top-tier Truth: *Face-to-face makes the difference.* The reason why this error persists nationwide among school leaders is that there is a subset of teachers for whom lengthy written evaluations are effective (just like there is a small group of learners for whom lengthy lectures are most effective). This leads to the dangerous conclusion that all teachers develop well by reading lengthy evaluations. In what other field do we subscribe to this idea?

Error 3: Just tell them; they'll get it.

Top-tier Truth: *If they don't do the thinking, they won't internalize what they learn.* In classroom instruction, highly effective teachers push the students to do the thinking. If teachers eclipse this thinking by providing conclusions or answers too quickly, students will disengage. Feedback is not any different: if teachers don't participate in the process of thinking about their teaching, they are less likely to internalize the feedback. This is metacognition applied to teacher development: having teachers think about their teaching improves their performance.

Error 4: State the concrete action step. Then the teacher will act.

Top-tier Truth: *Guided practice makes perfect.* If a surgeon simply tells a resident how to perform an operation, the resident will be less effective than if she practises with the surgeon's guidance. Teaching is the same: practising implementation of the feedback with the *leader* is at the heart of speeding up the improvement cycle. It also allows teachers to make mistakes before they're in front of the students again.

Error 5: Teachers can implement feedback at any time.

Top-tier Truth: *Nail down the timing.* Having a concrete timeline in which feedback will be implemented serves two purposes: it makes sure everyone has clear expectations as to when this will be accomplished and it will expose action steps that are not really able to be accomplished in a week.

Adapted from *Leverage Leadership*, by Paul Bambrick-Santoyo

Feedback tennis

1st point: Ace – positive feedback

2nd point: I'm curious about…

Return: You've got me thinking…
…or … that's a good question…

3rd point: Just tell them!

Reflection and goal-setting

Having accessed this content, what has resonated with you most strongly?

What do you want to do or change as a result?

What is the benefit for you of taking this action or making this change? Why do you want to do it?

How will you know if you have been successful?

Planning for your success

What's the timing? By when will you have achieved it?

_____
_____
_____
_____
_____
_____

What or who could support you making this happen?

_____
_____
_____
_____
_____

What or who could stop this happening?

_____
_____
_____
_____
_____

What can you do to prevent this?

_____
_____
_____
_____
_____
_____

What's your very first step to start this off? When will you take it?

Reviewing your success
What has changed for the better? What have you achieved?

Is there anything that you would like to further improve?

Notes

Topic 31: Appraisal meetings

If you are using the first or second edition of Leadership Matters, see the following page references for the related content: **LM1 no content LM2 pages 115-116**

Six key areas for leadership action

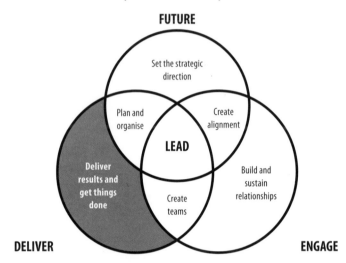

Twelve tips for great appraisal meetings

1. Agree time and place well in advance, **stick to these arrangements**, and be **well prepared** for the meeting.
2. Give the appraisee time to reflect on their goals and **rate themselves** in advance.
3. Ask them to also think about **areas for development** ahead of the meeting.
4. Wherever possible, give some **positive feedback** at the start.
5. Making sure you have **good evidence**, collected from a range of sources which has ideally been shared in advance.
6. There should be **no surprises**. If there are performance concerns, they should always be raised at the time they arise and support offered.
7. They should do more of the talking. **Ask good questions** to help them reflect for themselves on their strengths and areas for development.
8. Keep the meeting **appropriately formal**. It's not a social occasion and will usually matter a lot to the person being appraised. Take it seriously.
9. Take care in your write-up **not to over-praise or miss out concerns**. Both of these could come back to haunt you if performance dips.
10. Make sure new goals are **SMART** (specific, measurable, achievable, relevant and time-bound). Avoid setting goals that you both know will never be achieved.
11. Make sure you keep **good notes** and ask them to sign off (and comment, if they wish) on the final record of the meeting.
12. Ask for **feedback** on how you conducted the appraisal.

Reflection and goal-setting

Having accessed this content, what has resonated with you most strongly?

What do you want to do or change as a result?

What is the benefit for you of taking this action or making this change?
Why do you want to do it?

How will you know if you have been successful?

Planning for your success

What's the timing? By when will you have achieved it?

_____
_____
_____
_____
_____
_____
_____

What or who could support you making this happen?

_____
_____
_____
_____
_____
_____
_____

What or who could stop this happening?

_____
_____
_____
_____
_____
_____

What can you do to prevent this?

_____
_____
_____
_____
_____
_____
_____

What's your very first step to start this off? When will you take it?

Reviewing your success
What has changed for the better? What have you achieved?

Is there anything that you would like to further improve?

Notes

Topic 32: Difficult conversations

If you are using the first or second edition of Leadership Matters, see the following page references for the related content: **LM1 pages 129-133 LM2 pages 142-149**

Please note this topic has two videos (32a and 32b)

NEFI ART

1. **N**ame the issue
2. Describe a specific **E**xample
3. Describe your **F**eelings about the issue
4. Clarify what is at stake, why this is **I**mportant
5. **A**ccept your contribution to this problem
6. Indicate your wish to **R**esolve the issue
7. Invite **T**hem to respond.

Useful strategies

1. Don't get side-tracked into other issues
2. Don't get into and argument
3. Respond to anger with calm gestures – lower voice, speak quietly and slowly
4. Try the last word or key word strategy
5. Respond to tears with silence
6. Do not try to physically comfort the person
7. Find the right time and place
8. Make a note of the discussion. Seek agreement on contents.

Reflection and goal-setting

Having accessed this content, what has resonated with you most strongly?

What do you want to do or change as a result?

What is the benefit for you of taking this action or making this change? Why do you want to do it?

How will you know if you have been successful?

Planning for your success

What's the timing? By when will you have achieved it?

What or who could support you making this happen?

What or who could stop this happening?

What can you do to prevent this?

What's your very first step to start this off? When will you take it?

Reviewing your success
What has changed for the better? What have you achieved?

Is there anything that you would like to further improve?

Notes

Topic 33: Prioritisation

If you are using the first or second edition of Leadership Matters, see the following page references for the related content: **LM1 pages 148-154 LM2 pages 163-169**

A model for prioritisation

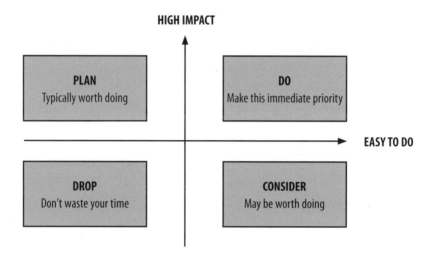

Carrying out a MICK review

More	What is working well that we should do more of?
Include	What would help us achieve our goals that we don't currently do?
Change	What do we do that is important but not quite working at the moment?
Kick-out	What do we do at the moment that we could probably manage without?

Reflection and goal-setting

Having accessed this content, what has resonated with you most strongly?

What do you want to do or change as a result?

What is the benefit for you of taking this action or making this change? Why do you want to do it?

How will you know if you have been successful?

Planning for your success

What's the timing? By when will you have achieved it?

What or who could support you making this happen?

What or who could stop this happening?

What can you do to prevent this?

What's your very first step to start this off? When will you take it?

_____
_____
_____
_____
_____
_____

Reviewing your success
What has changed for the better? What have you achieved?

_____
_____
_____
_____
_____

Is there anything that you would like to further improve?

_____
_____
_____
_____
_____
_____

Notes

Topic 34: Managing change

If you are using the first or second edition of Leadership Matters, see the following page references for the related content: **LM1 pages 137-142 LM2 pages 151-162**

Eight steps of chaange

John Kotter

Dimensions of change

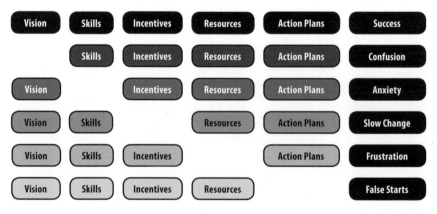

Knoster, Thousand and Villa

Reflection and goal-setting

Having accessed this content, what has resonated with you most strongly?

What do you want to do or change as a result?

What is the benefit for you of taking this action or making this change?
Why do you want to do it?

How will you know if you have been successful?

Planning for your success

What's the timing? By when will you have achieved it?

What or who could support you making this happen?

What or who could stop this happening?

What can you do to prevent this?

What's your very first step to start this off? When will you take it?

_____
_____
_____
_____
_____
_____

Reviewing your success
What has changed for the better? What have you achieved?

_____
_____
_____
_____
_____
_____

Is there anything that you would like to further improve?

_____
_____
_____
_____
_____
_____

Notes

Topic 35: Checklists

If you are using the first or second edition of Leadership Matters, see the following page references for the related content: **LM1 no content LM2 pages 156-157**

Parents' evening checklist

Action	Done	Notes
Check rooms booked		
Write to parents		
Talk to pupils in assembly		
Set up appointment system		
Organise room requirements with caretakers		
Ensure tutor team are briefed		
Organise student helpers		
Liaise with parents' association		
Remind staff of protocols regarding keeping to time and late-comers		
Organise evaluation forms		

An example of a checklist for change

Action	When	Notes
Be clear why change needed – get people wanting change		
Get a small group working on it and review the evidence of what works		
Create a draft vision and proposal		
Test it out with people		
Make sure everything is in place (especially skills and time to do it)		
Launch		
Ensure quick wins		
Get real-time feedback		
Challenge those not adopting		
Build into standard routines for planning and evaluation		

Reflection and goal-setting

Having accessed this content, what has resonated with you most strongly?

What do you want to do or change as a result?

What is the benefit for you of taking this action or making this change? Why do you want to do it?

How will you know if you have been successful?

Planning for your success

What's the timing? By when will you have achieved it?

What or who could support you making this happen?

What or who could stop this happening?

What can you do to prevent this?

What's your very first step to start this off? When will you take it?

_____

_____

_____

_____

_____

_____

Reviewing your success
What has changed for the better? What have you achieved?

_____

_____

_____

_____

_____

_____

Is there anything that you would like to further improve?

_____

_____

_____

_____

_____

_____

Notes

Topic 36: Personal organisation

There is no content in the first and second editions of
Leadership Matters that relates to this topic.

How to annoy people

Late to meetings or with deadlines	**Don't stick to what was agreed**
Leave people out of the loop	**Ask for feedback and then ignore it**
Rushed delegation or decisions	**Be slow or never reply to emails**

- ✓ Have one place you use for 'action collection'
- ✓ Empty circles technique
- ✓ Do immediately **OR**
- ✓ Transfer to your main electronic to-do list
- ✓ Make sure it allows you to re-prioritise easily
- ✓ Important to only have **ONE** to-do list
- ✓ Many jobs arrive as email so double-up
- ✓ Email title as task
- ✓ You only need five folders
- ✓ Now – Inbox & A
- ✓ Soon – A & B
- ✓ Later – C

Reflection and goal-setting

Having accessed this content, what has resonated with you most strongly?

_____
_____
_____
_____
_____
_____

What do you want to do or change as a result?

_____
_____
_____
_____
_____
_____
_____

What is the benefit for you of taking this action or making this change?
Why do you want to do it?

_____
_____
_____
_____
_____
_____
_____

How will you know if you have been successful?

_____
_____
_____
_____
_____
_____

Planning for your success
What's the timing? By when will you have achieved it?

What or who could support you making this happen?

What or who could stop this happening?

What can you do to prevent this?

What's your very first step to start this off? When will you take it?

_____
_____
_____
_____
_____
_____

Reviewing your success
What has changed for the better? What have you achieved?

_____
_____
_____
_____
_____
_____

Is there anything that you would like to further improve?

_____
_____
_____
_____
_____
_____

Notes

Topic 37: Leadership styles

If you are using the first or second edition of Leadership Matters, see the following page references for the related content: **LM1 pages 157-162 LM2 pages 173-178**

Summary of different leadership styles and when to use them

Style	Description	When useful	Correlation
Visionary	Communicating the goal; expectations on delivery	Pretty much anytime; set pieces and 1:1 dialogue	+0.54
Affiliative	Building and sustaining relationships	Again, always useful but especially if morale poor	+0.46
Directive	Telling people what to do, often in detail	Low capability or competence; no time	-0.26
Democratic	Sharing decision-making; delegating power	Confidence in the team; more time available	+0.43
Pacesetting	Copy me and keep up with me	When need fast change; show what's possible	-0.25
Coaching	Asking questions; focus on developing others	When you have time to build capacity in others	+0.42

Based on Goleman

Changing leadership style over time

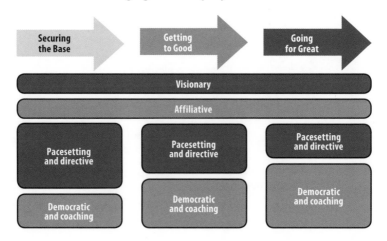

Reflection and goal-setting

Having accessed this content, what has resonated with you most strongly?

What do you want to do or change as a result?

What is the benefit for you of taking this action or making this change?
Why do you want to do it?

How will you know if you have been successful?

Planning for your success

What's the timing? By when will you have achieved it?

What or who could support you making this happen?

What or who could stop this happening?

What can you do to prevent this?

What's your very first step to start this off? When will you take it?

Reviewing your success
What has changed for the better? What have you achieved?

Is there anything that you would like to further improve?

Notes

Topic 38: Ask first

If you are using the first or second edition of Leadership Matters, see the following page references for the related content: **LM1 pages 171-176 LM2 pages 189-192**

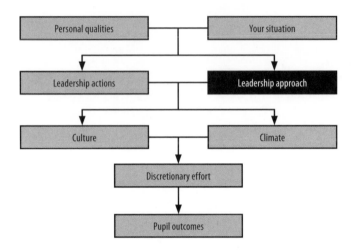

Ask First

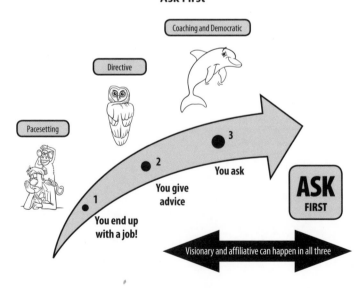

Reflection and goal-setting

Having accessed this content, what has resonated with you most strongly?

What do you want to do or change as a result?

What is the benefit for you of taking this action or making this change?
Why do you want to do it?

How will you know if you have been successful?

Planning for your success

What's the timing? By when will you have achieved it?

_____

_____

_____

_____

_____

_____

What or who could support you making this happen?

_____

_____

_____

_____

_____

_____

What or who could stop this happening?

_____

_____

_____

_____

_____

_____

What can you do to prevent this?

_____

_____

_____

_____

_____

_____

What's your very first step to start this off? When will you take it?

Reviewing your success

What has changed for the better? What have you achieved?

Is there anything that you would like to further improve?

Notes

Topic 39: Coaching approach

If you are using the first or second edition of Leadership Matters, see the following page references for the related content: **LM1 no content LM2 pages 192-193**

The coaching continuum

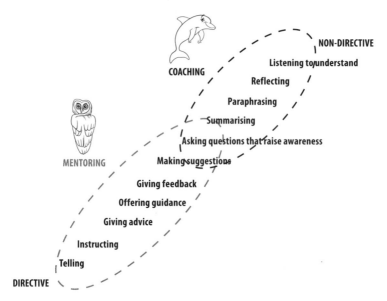

Adapted from Myles Downey

A definition of coaching

Coaching definition

A one-to-one conversation that focuses on the enhancement of **learning** and **development** through increasing **self-awareness** and a sense of personal **responsibility**, where the coach facilitates the **self-directed** learning of the coachee, through **questioning**, active **listening** and appropriate **challenge** in a **supportive** and encouraging environment.

Campbell and van Nieuwerburgh

Reflection and goal-setting

Having accessed this content, what has resonated with you most strongly?

What do you want to do or change as a result?

What is the benefit for you of taking this action or making this change? Why do you want to do it?

How will you know if you have been successful?

Planning for your success

What's the timing? By when will you have achieved it?

_____

_____

_____

_____

_____

_____

What or who could support you making this happen?

_____

_____

_____

_____

_____

_____

What or who could stop this happening?

_____

_____

_____

_____

_____

_____

What can you do to prevent this?

_____

_____

_____

_____

_____

_____

What's your very first step to start this off? When will you take it?

_____
_____
_____
_____
_____
_____

Reviewing your success
What has changed for the better? What have you achieved?

_____
_____
_____
_____
_____

Is there anything that you would like to further improve?

_____
_____
_____
_____
_____
_____

Notes

Topic 40: GROWTH coaching

If you are using the first or second edition of Leadership Matters, see the following page references for the related content: **LM1 no content LM2 pages 192-200**

The GROWTH Coaching Model

Growth Coaching International

Reflection and goal-setting

Having accessed this content, what has resonated with you most strongly?

What do you want to do or change as a result?

What is the benefit for you of taking this action or making this change? Why do you want to do it?

How will you know if you have been successful?

Planning for your success

What's the timing? By when will you have achieved it?

_____

_____

_____

_____

_____

_____

_____

What or who could support you making this happen?

_____

_____

_____

_____

_____

_____

What or who could stop this happening?

_____

_____

_____

_____

_____

_____

What can you do to prevent this?

_____

_____

_____

_____

_____

_____

What's your very first step to start this off? When will you take it?

_____

_____

_____

_____

_____

_____

Reviewing your success
What has changed for the better? What have you achieved?

_____

_____

_____

_____

_____

Is there anything that you would like to further improve?

_____

_____

_____

_____

_____

Notes

LM Persona

Reflection and goal-setting

Having completed LM Persona, what three things are you most pleased to discover?

Is there anything specific that you have identified about yourself that you think it would be useful to share with your peers, team members or line manager?

Is there anything you think you might like to work on being more effective at?

What is the benefit for you of taking this action or making this change? Why do you want to do it?

How will you know if you have been successful?

Planning for your success

What's the timing? By when will you have achieved it?

What or who could support you making this happen?

What or who could stop this happening?

What can you do to prevent this?

What's your very first step to start this off? When will you take it?

Review of your success

What has changed for the better? What have you achieved?

Is there anything that you would like to further improve?

LM 360

Reflection and goal-setting

Having completed LM 360, what three things are you most pleased to discover?

_____

_____

_____

_____

_____

_____

_____

Is there anything you think you might like to work on being more effective at?

_____

_____

_____

_____

_____

_____

_____

What is the benefit for you of taking this action or making this change? Why do you want to do it?

_____

_____

_____

_____

_____

_____

How will you know if you have been successful?

Planning for your success

What's the timing? By when will you have achieved it?

What or who could support you making this happen?

What or who could stop this happening?

What can you do to prevent this?

What's your very first step to start this off? When will you take it?

Review of your success

What has changed for the better? What have you achieved?

Is there anything that you would like to further improve?

LM Style

Reflection and goal-setting

Having completed LM Style, what three things are you most pleased to discover?

_____

_____

_____

_____

_____

_____

Is there anything you think you might like to work on being more effective at?

_____

_____

_____

_____

_____

_____

What is the benefit for you of taking this action or making this change? Why do you want to do it?

_____

_____

_____

_____

_____

_____

How will you know if you have been successful?

_____

Planning for your success

What's the timing? By when will you have achieved it?

_____

What or who could support you making this happen?

_____

What or who could stop this happening?

_____

What can you do to prevent this?

What's your very first step to start this off? When will you take it?

Review of your success

What has changed for the better? What have you achieved?

Is there anything that you would like to further improve?

Checklist for change

Action	When	Notes
Be clear why change needed – get people wanting change		
Get a small group working on it and review the evidence of what works		
Create a draft vision and proposal		
Test it out with people		
Make sure everything is in place (especially skills and time to do it)		
Launch		
Ensure quick wins		
Get real-time feedback		
Challenge those not adopting		
Build into standard routines for planning and evaluation		

Checklist for change

Action	When	Notes
Be clear why change needed – get people wanting change		
Get a small group working on it and review the evidence of what works		
Create a draft vision and proposal		
Test it out with people		
Make sure everything is in place (especially skills and time to do it)		
Launch		
Ensure quick wins		
Get real-time feedback		
Challenge those not adopting		
Build into standard routines for planning and evaluation		

Checklist for change

Action	When	Notes
Be clear why change needed – get people wanting change		
Get a small group working on it and review the evidence of what works		
Create a draft vision and proposal		
Test it out with people		
Make sure everything is in place (especially skills and time to do it)		
Launch		
Ensure quick wins		
Get real-time feedback		
Challenge those not adopting		
Build into standard routines for planning and evaluation		

Checklist for change

Action	When	Notes
Be clear why change needed – get people wanting change		
Get a small group working on it and review the evidence of what works		
Create a draft vision and proposal		
Test it out with people		
Make sure everything is in place (especially skills and time to do it)		
Launch		
Ensure quick wins		
Get real-time feedback		
Challenge those not adopting		
Build into standard routines for planning and evaluation		

Checklist for change

Action	When	Notes
Be clear why change needed – get people wanting change		
Get a small group working on it and review the evidence of what works		
Create a draft vision and proposal		
Test it out with people		
Make sure everything is in place (especially skills and time to do it)		
Launch		
Ensure quick wins		
Get real-time feedback		
Challenge those not adopting		
Build into standard routines for planning and evaluation		

Notes

ISBN 978-1-911382-90-4

John Catt Educational Limited
15 Riduna Park
Station Road,
Melton, Woodbridge,
Suffolk IP12 1QT
01394 389850
enquiries@johncatt.com
www.johncatt.com